MW01153134

RAINBOW WIZARD
Everything for Kids

Copyright © 2021

All rights reserved. No part of this publication may be reproduced, stored in retrieval system, or transmitted in any form or by any means, electronic, mechanical, photocopying, recording or otherwise without the prior written permission of the publisher.

Publication by Rainbow Wizard

This Book Belongs to:

....

....

If you are looking for a coloring book for older kids, then check it out:

BO8NF32FS1

Or type ASIN in amazon search bar ↑

All Departments ▾	BO8NF32FS1	🔍

ASIN: BO8NJR5FPY

SCAN a QR CODE

ASIN: BO8NJR53L4

SCAN a QR CODE

ASIN: BO8P3PC5ZJ

COLORING BOOK WITH
ANIMALS – ALPHABET – WORDS

Baby Coloring Book 1 Year

SCAN a QR CODE
OR TYPE IN AMAZON SEARCH BAR

BO979JFVTD

Baby Coloring Book 2 Years

BO979V2ZRH

Toddler Coloring Book

BO979ZJ58S

Thank you

Just a note to say thank you your purchase from me.
I hope you enjoyed my product as much as I have enjoyed creating it.

If you want:

1. You can leave a review under this book on Amazon.

2. You can check out my other books by scan the QR Code on the back cover.

3. You can follow my profile on Amazon and get New Releases.

4. You can check RainbowWizardBooks.com and discover more books.

RAINBOW WIZARD
Everything for Kids

Contact me:

rainbowwizardbooks@gmail.com

Made in the USA
Monee, IL
09 October 2024

67508759R00061